Walking on the Shores of Heaven

A Cancer Survivor's View of the Other Side

Walking on the Shores
of Heaven

A Cancer Survivor's View of the Other Side

Rex Vesey

Interpretive Illustrations
by
Charlie Wolfsandle

Cover illustration by Charlie Wolfsandle

Cover design by Charlie Wolfsandle and Ryan Belnap

R & R Publications
Flagstaff, Arizona
LouellaHolter.com

This book is dedicated to all MD Anderson staff members, their patients, families, and everyone who desires hope and solace beyond life's passage.

GOD LOVES YOU

Acknowledgments

My acknowledgments must begin with an unending thanks encompassed by the deepest heartfelt gratitude to the mega-powerful, loving "Presence" that runs the universe. Without a connection to the living light of this "Presence" I would not have been able to experience anything in my mind's viewing screen. Awareness of this connection has brought me to an appreciation level I never before thought possible. This "Presence" is the source of all meaning.

For transforming my written descriptions into wonderful illustrations, I wish to greatly commend Charlie Wolfsandle, who spent many hours with me creating a visual semblance of each vision. He had the challenging task of creatively interpreting my written descriptions into visual form. The end result was 12 beautiful renderings worthy of individual meditation.

For publication, I wish to especially acknowledge and commend my friend and publishing agent Louella Holter. This book was easy for me to publish because of her kind, competent, and persistent efforts. She understands personally how a transforming event can affect one's life; her book *Bikes, Dreams, and the Inner Life* describes her own personally transforming life event.

For original proofreading, word processing, and clarity of expression, I owe a sincere thanks to my young friend Manisha Master, who has excelled in her studies at Arizona State University.

A very special acknowledgment of thanks is needed for Malcolm Smith, Spiritual Healer, who has helped me to be more open to the flow of spiritual energy for many years.

Finally, a very, very special thank you to my wife Lynn, whose endearing and enduring patience, love, and support have helped me to continually grow as a person, while pursuing the path of spiritual questing.

Contents

Introduction

During the Christmas holidays in 2006, it suddenly occurred to me that I should buy a blank notebook from Barnes & Noble. I was in a very anxious state of mind; I was waiting at home in Scottsdale for the results of biopsies from my urologist, who had sent them to a California lab.

On December 26th, an associate of my urologist phoned me with the news that I had prostate cancer. After further tests, my urologist determined that the cancer was advanced, but localized. My anxiety rose further when he explained that I needed an operation immediately.

The shock of this news sent me reeling with indecision, and fear of impending death. I contacted both of my daughters for support and advice on how to proceed. Heather and Mareli and their husbands were very supportive; they strongly advised me to seek help from the top cancer center in the country—this led me to the MD Anderson Cancer Center, in Houston. So I gathered all my medical records, and then my wife and I flew to Texas.

My wife and daughters contacted nearly 100 relatives and friends to pray for my full recovery. On February 5th, 2007, I had a very successful prostatectomy. After the removal of all suspect surrounding tissues and glands, test results showed that no other areas were affected. However, continued periodical testing was required to make sure my body remained free of cancer.

It was during the first two weeks of recovery, when I was visiting the MD Anderson Cancer Center emergency room, that a change came over me. I sensed that those around me, who were experiencing great pain and suffering, were receiving strength from some distant reality. I believed that I was also receiving strength from a distant reality, from the many people who were praying for me to recover quickly and become cancer free. This visit was a very psychologically changing and spiritually awakening experience.

All of this wonderful spiritual energy coming my way helped to promote the process of being able to visualize a number of beautiful places in realms beyond our world. As I engaged in regular meditation in the months following my recovery, twelve vivid, beautiful images of wonderful places lying beyond this reality were brought into focus for me, and I recorded them in the notebook. After carefully study-ing these descriptions, my artist-illustrator took on the challenging task of providing the best possible artistic semblance of what I had sensed and observed. I have described these to the best of my ability in this text.

The primary purpose of these visual representa-tions is to aid the reader in developing a mental picture of each vision. The renderings are not to be an endpoint for the reader's imagination, but rather a beginning, for I believe the power of visioning lies in each one of us. My verbal descriptions could never do justice to what I saw, so these representations have been included to enrich the reader's enjoyment of the mystical visions and to spark further imagination.

Seeing mental pictures has become a common mind-event in my life. For the past 35 years, I have experienced mental images in the front part of my forehead after studying handwritten signatures. These images were life segments of those who gave me permission to read their interests and personality traits from a concentrated viewing of their signatures.

While I have seen mental pictures in the past, the images that I received following my surgery were unlike any previous visions I've ever had. A serious illness such as cancer can have a tremendous impact on all aspects of one's life. According to the University of Texas MD Anderson Cancer Center Communications Office, there can be "emotional, psychological, social, spiritual, legal, and practical" challenges. "They can be pertinent whether you are recently diagnosed, in the midst of treatment, a survivor, or a caregiver."[1]

I believe that what we can picture in our minds may be a breakthrough to a much larger reality—a reality that theoretical physics is attempting to tap into. As an example, scientists designing the world's largest collider, the Hadron, say, "The collider may be powerful enough to test one of the most bizarre predictions of string theory—that there are many dimensions out there."[2]

Heaven, I believe, is a vast network of energy bands or beltways, which are in a continuously evolving state, containing harmonic vibrations much like overtones on a musical scale. These are resonating

---

[1] Sandi Stromberg, "Beyond the Medical: Other Dimensions of Care," *Network* (University of Texas, M.D. Anderson Cancer Center, Fall 2008).
[2] Michio Kako, "Testing String Theory," *Discover* August 2005, 34.

from possibly three prime energy sources fused together into a central column or core pulsating out in all directions, much like a broadcast sphere of masterful intelligence and infinite energy. We are all part of this energy, and in the energy state beyond the death of our three-dimensional bodies we will be able to explore the many mansions or dimensions in God's house. As spoken by the great prophet, healer, and teacher Jesus, "In my Father's house are many mansions."

Our challenge and wonderful opportunity is to create auric energy keys to harmonize our soul vibrations to enter through the shimmering energy vestibules into these dimensions. Many believe lifetimes of learning are needed, but perhaps not. I hesitate to make any judgment on this, and will leave the matter for other writers to discuss. As to a method of practice to achieve a state of higher vibrational energy or higher levels of consciousness, I again leave this to more qualified writers. Wayne Dyer and Pir Vilayat Inayat Khan readily come to mind, along with so many who have interpreted the Cayce readings and the *Course in Miracles*.

The goal of this book is to describe the visions I received from what I believe to be areas of Heaven. Heaven has become a wonderful, exciting quest for me. Concentrated, directed, thought-forming "one-point" meditation, as utilized in the field of dowsing, transported my mind into what I call the "White Field." This is the zone of bright white energy that transmitted images of places from beyond into my mind. These images began to appear much like viewing a beautiful painting. As the images unfolded, more detail became apparent, similar to focusing a tele-photo lens on a camera.

Describing these visions has been very challeng-ing, as words cannot do justice to the images. I feel extremely humbled to have had these visions. To touch the infinite from the finite was indeed a rare privilege and the greatest honor for me. I am re-minded of the Bible passage in Luke 17, verse 21, which states, "The Kingdom of God is within you."

It is up to us to find the keys to unlock the doors to greater levels of consciousness, to experience the most wonderful companionship of walking into new realities with those in harmony with the Creative Forces, where God's love is pulsating everywhere. I have designated the following twelve visions "Ever-Views," as they appear firm and lasting in my mind.

For to Awaken in Life We Must First Awaken Beyond Life
– Pir Vilayat Inayat Khan

Vision 1

Reunions in the White Mist

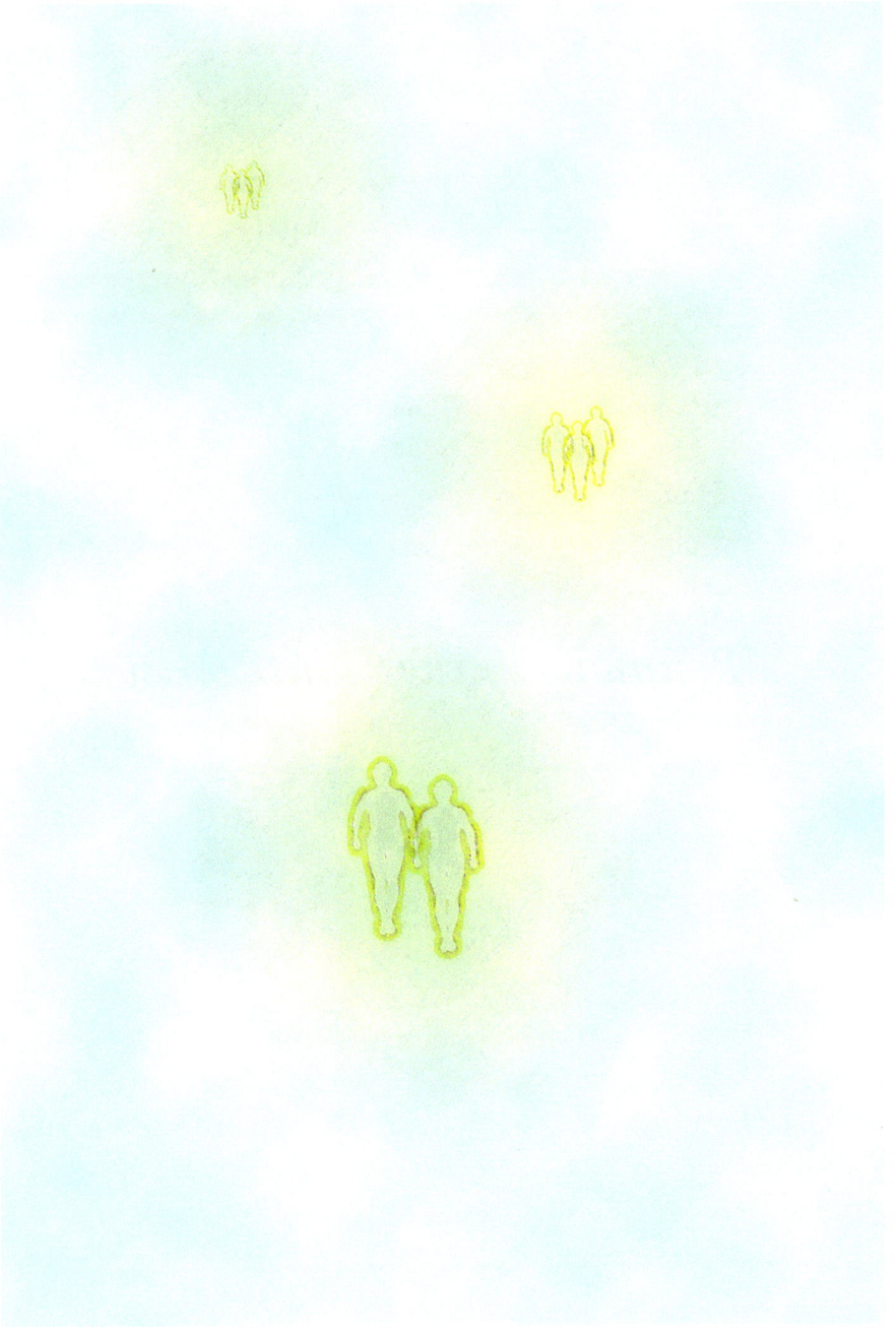

Reunions in the White Mist

The white mist appears to be a soul barrier in this vision, which you can only cross into if it is your time to cross over; therefore, only viewing at a distance is possible. This is true of all the visions described in this text; they are views perhaps similar to remote viewing, yet your "Essence Self" has not left where you are.

One very special person or a small group of relatives or friends may come into the mist to meet you. My vision did not indicate whether this meeting takes place before or after the counseling session in Counselor Hall (described in Vision 3). Neither did it indicate whether that special loved one or group guides you to Counselor Hall, nor whether the greeter is your Counselor of Light. From reading several books on near-death experiences, it appears all possibilities exist.

In this vision, I could see many people joyously embracing, crying with joy, and discovering they were in a renewed state of existence, fully conscious of what they were experi-encing. This crossing over was an experience of ecstasy which filled their whole soul beings with energy—energy that would help them explore the wondrous beauty in the dimensions of Heaven.

Vision 2

Stairway to Archways of Golden White Light

Stairway to Archways of Golden White Light

This vision brought me into view of a stairway of glistening steps enveloped by a cloudy energy mist. The stairs were very expansive in appearance, with wide steps that faded into the moving energy mist. The staircase curved slightly as it wound upwards. As I ascended, archways appeared on each side.

The archways were sparkling white, with a shimmering, golden white curtain of energy vibrating between them. In this vision, I was not able to enter any of the arched portals. I received the impression that they might be connected to places from other planetary systems, where souls were climbing stairways of energy just like the one I was ascending.

The termination point of the stairways was a hall of great expanse, which I have designated, "Counselor Hall." This is described in the next vision.

Vision 3

Counselor Hall

Counselor Hall

This vision is characterized by a huge hall of great expanse, containing a myriad of alcoves furnished with glowing tables of light. Seated behind these tables are highly developed soul entities dedicated to radiating personal warmth, empathy, compassionate understanding, and love to each soul who enters. Each soul apparently feels a strong compulsion to meet with one or more of these counselors. Contoured chairs composed of semi-solid, semi-translucent energy are available. These are situated across from the tables, which glow as stabilized light beams.

The "Soul Counselors" have the sole desire to help all entities create a personal growth plan from a total life review, and to discuss options that will harmonize their soul vibrations with the "Central Soul" in the universe (God).

During the counseling process, the counselor helps the individual to reflect upon and evaluate images of his or her life. This is done in an extremely kind, non-directive manner, with no judgment brought in on the part of the counselor. The individual can see alternative possibilities leading to different outcomes if a different choice had been made. Choice is the chief determinant.

This review is a self-judgment process made easy for the participant by the great personal warmth and compassionate understanding of the counselor. I could not determine how long this process takes, for time as we know it here in our three-dimensional plane appears not to exist there. Many levels of vibrating fields form the essence of substance in the place I envisioned. Since we are also in an energy state, what we experience there seems solid to semi-solid to our soul selves.

Vision 4

Gardens of Reflection and Repose

Gardens of Reflection and Repose

Soon after the passing of a family member or friend, I have seen them walking in this verdant place. It appears to have many types of landscapes adjoined by intricate walkways and is covered with flowering plants and trees of indescribable beauty.

This is a recurring vision in my life. Most often, it includes couples who have recently been reunited where previously one of them had passed over. They all appear to be of an age between twenty and forty years. Occasionally, single persons are found there in a meditative walk, along with children happily wading in shallow streams, observing and smelling the wide array of flowering plants.

This verdant environment appears to have species unknown to Earth. What was particularly interesting was that each species seemed to harmonize and enhance the health, growth, and beauty of those around it in an exchange of life energy.

In this vision, animal life appeared to be absent except for birds. I have not received any visions of the place of repose of other fauna, but I feel strongly that it exists, and that there are multiple levels of animal soul interactions.

The time spent in the gardens for personal reflection provided one with a great appreciation for living flora. What was so wonderful was that the "Love of God" radiated from each plant and tree, filling one's spirit body with warm, vibrant, loving energy. This energy empowered each spirit body with a greater capacity to love.

Vision 5

Groves of Endless Spring

Groves of Endless Spring

In this vision, I emerged from the "White Field" to view beautiful groves of blossoming trees. These groves stretched endlessly into a multi-hued horizon. The blossoms far outnumbered the leaves on the branches of the trees. The groves were arranged in rows stretching up and down on low hills leading into valleys, which blended into one horizon after the other. Between the flowering trees flowing into the valleys was bright, vibrant grass, which changed in hues of green as one wandered among the groves with a light, drifting walk.

As flowers floated down from the trees, they were immediately replaced by new sprouts on the branches. The fallen blossoms formed a beautiful fabric walkway amidst the soft grass of emerging green. From a distance, it appeared to be a beautiful landscape painting with an endless perspective.

If you wish to leave this beautiful area of blossoming trees, as with other areas you are experiencing in Heaven, you will it so. You are then moved along by a field of force either back to the central vestibule of entrance ways to other heavenly settings, or past the horizon of the present one. There appear to be mystical energy zones one passes through to arrive at the next setting, as I have described in several of these visions.

Vision 6

Villages of Enhanced Earthly Design

Villages of Enhanced Earthly Design

As this vision came into focus from my meditating process, a grand country setting opened up. It was dotted with villages representing every period of history. The villages comprised shops and homes beautifully positioned among valleys and rolling, grassy hills. Tree clusters of many varieties were interspersed throughout the communities. All architectural styles experienced on Earth existed in the dwelling designs.

There were religious edifices endemic to each belief system or religion of the soul beings living in a particular village. Souls of similar religious interests, socio-cultural backgrounds, and belief systems enjoyed associating with each other in their respective neighborhoods. Interpersonal harmony was the goal of all living there, and loving tolerance for different viewpoints was found everywhere.

I did not see cities in this vision, but later I describe one I saw in another vision, which I have designated "The City of Spires."

In speculating on how the content of Heaven is created, I believe it is being formed, at least partially, now, by the thoughts and desires of those living in the Earth-plane. The quality of their Heaven will be based on the quality of their thoughts and desires. I do not choose to define what "quality" is, because that would entail a personal judgment, which I'm continually trying to free myself from to aid my own spiritual growth.

I also believe those of similar thought or cognitive styles will be comfortably attracted to each other as soul beings in Heaven, and will greatly enjoy planning new spiritual communities where personal growth can be further enhanced.

Vision 7

Cathedral of Choirs

Cathedral of Choirs

This vision is especially unique in that sounds of great power resounded in my consciousness. From a building standpoint, this vision may have been called "Rainbow Cathedral." It was a massive structure of interlocking archways of rainbow lights fused together to form chambers of shimmering, soft-glowing fields of light energy; these were surrounded by wisps of moving pure white clouds.

The structure was set alone and surrounded by what appeared to be a type of short green grass, but of an unknown substance, stretching out in all directions. It had the property of efflorescence in color change, relating to all tints of green, and appeared to have internal luminosity.

The joy upon entering this place penetrated your whole being. It felt like convulsive energy pounding inside your total essence, filling it with exhilaration beyond description. It was so transforming that everyone who entered became bright white in appearance, like they were wearing a special robe of glowing white light. You felt so much joy from the choral music coming forth that you wanted to embrace everyone you encountered as a loving friend. You could also find a group singing, join in, and instantly know the words coming to you from an unknown source. The "essence of God" was in those chorales, refining your spiritual body, mind, and soul.

It was wonderful to see that the universe is run by a "Grand Harmonic Composer." True mystics have without a doubt been able to tune into this "grand harmonic essence" and impart to us beautiful pathways for spiritual growth. I believe our goal is to tune in with this great creative pattern and "Soul of the Universe." This attunement is the spiritual process at its best.

The chorales of praise being sung by the myriad of voices were the "songs of God" and did not seem to represent any particular religion. The beautiful interchange of loving energy vibrating in those chorales served to transform all who participated with new purpose and joyous insight.

Vision 8

City of Spires

City of Spires

In this vision, the "City of Spires" appeared as a cluster of structures of great expanse. These included private retreat quarters, libraries, laboratories, lecture halls, and personal development centers, which were interconnected to open gardens and arched corridors leading to auditoriums.

There were colleges for every type of personal study interest imaginable. These comprised universities for learning on a massive scale, the spires being towers of central auditoriums.

From the interior of these central auditoriums were atriums leading to special interest and talent development centers. These centers were specialized colleges focusing on particular fields of knowledge. For example, if one was interested in music, every aspect of the musical field was available for exploration, from composing to instrumentation, to vocal and orchestral participation. Doorways led to special practice and performance areas.

Of particular interest to me was that there was a College of Creativity, which explored such fields of study as the science of meaning, the science of aesthetics, and the science of planning for new creation. Creativity was, however, valued as a pursuit in all colleges of study.

Notably absent among the fields of study were business and economics. There may have been other fields of study also absent, but I was unable to determine them in this vision.

Vision 9

Temple of Harmonic Attunement

Temple of Harmonic Attunement

This outstanding vision brought into view an amazing temple. The temple was a multi-faceted group of spires joined by ribbed archways with open corridors on all sides. Lights, changing in hues of all the colors found in the human aura, illuminated the whole of the interior. Light rays streamed out through the archways with iridescent beauty. There were beautiful flowered walkways leading to the arched openings, where energy transformers emitted beautiful harmonic sounds.

In an unknown manner, I sensed a telepathic message being sent out to all those approaching this temple. It seemed to say, "Those may enter who seek to attune their spiritual soul body vibrations in harmony to the 'prime vibrations.'" These prime vibrations were being emitted all over this beautiful structure. It felt like a pulse energy source of all life, so alive that the energy waves themselves contained intelligent thought that was aware of all existence everywhere in the universe.

The intense rapture of this temple made one feel that God's love is always here, and everywhere in the universe. This vision truly brought into focus the sacredness and excellence of our inner being.

Vision 10

Guilds of Infinite Wisdom

Guilds of Infinite Wisdom

The setting for this vision featured gardens enclosed with columns geometrically placed within intersecting triangles and semi-circles. Atriums were formed between the columns, which contained no roof structure, giving it a large pavilion appearance. Conference tables surrounded by large, flat-backed chairs were interspersed throughout these atriums. Wide walkways were delineated by flowering low bushes and flower beds brimming with blossoms. These were brilliant yellow-gold, red-orange, and turquoise in color.

Within this spacious, open setting people gathered to visit, talk, and collect knowledge of interest from various groups of master teachers who had experience with vast numbers of planetary systems in the universe. Visitors could pose questions to these wise master teachers knowing they would receive answers in a kind, loving manner which would expand their consciousness.

This group of master teachers I designated the "Guilds of Infinite Wisdom," because their goal was to further spiritual transcendency and existential aesthetics in those seeking higher spiritual knowledge. The spiritual content explored in the dialogue between the masters and the participants centered on deriving reverential meaning from the God-Force present in the creative process of producing new galaxies and new worlds.

This would include a myriad of opportunities for souls to make spiritual choices on how to provide service and continue building spiritual communities in those worlds. The process goal would be to create a perfected existence there for eternal life in the next dimension. The freeing of spiritual potentialities and existential excellence is the central focus and goal of the "Guilds of Infinite Wisdom." Soul guidance is the primary role of the spiritual masters.

Vision 11

Fountain of Chimes

Fountain of Chimes

The visualization of this heavenly phenomenon was truly awe-inspiring. Like all the visions described in this book, words can only provide a partial semblance of its beauty and power of being.

It was a towering, polylithic, translucent structure of interlocking crystals surrounded by clouds of energy, which were in intermixing layers. These fluctuated in size as the crystalline structure glowed in various parts with various colors of the spectrum. The energy clouds appeared to be held in place by an invisible containment field.

As one's soul self approached, energy particles showered out of the clouds. They were amorphous in form, and took on the colors in the auric field of the soul's spiritual body. They might appropriately be called energy flakes. As one approached the fountain, one's whole being was completely filled with what sounded like a massive choir of chimes. These chimes pulsated in full harmony throughout one's whole being. The feeling is one of pure ecstasy, like a beautiful anthem resounding inside you.

This beautification experience gave you the intuitive feeling that you were connected to God, the "prime source of all being." This fountain made you so graciously thankful that you were created to feel such joy and bliss in being self-aware and sentient to experience the living exultance of God's presence.

Vision 12

Colonnade of Soul Projection

Colonnade of Soul Projection

This vision encompassed views of a place where blinding white light energy was emitted in all directions from spiraling energy columns. This collection of columns appeared to be composed of stationary energy fields, which pulsated internally, emitting flowering tongues of beautiful flames from their apex points. These extended upwards, fusing into what became beams of energy spinning around at 360 degrees, and then shooting off like energy sparks from a grinding wheel into dimensions unseen.

Surrounding this massive array of columns were gathering halls, within which appeared to be shining walkways supported by energy fields that led to round enclosed chambers. I surmised that these were soul compression and projection chambers where one's soul self could be sent into other dimensions or worlds.

Souls came voluntarily to this place when they felt their soul harmonics were at the right key level to enter another existence for continued spiritual growth. It appeared that groups of souls could go together to these other worlds or return back to the Earth-plane for further development. I received the impression that the great gift of free will which we all have provides us with wonderful opportunities to choose our spiritual sojourns. These will guide us toward the level of spiritual development we seek. Having the opportunity to choose the roles and experiences in our coming life is what I believe to be the highest form of grace.

The grand Colonnade of Soul Projection, like all places described in these twelve visions, radiated with wonderful warmth of acceptance, joy, and love. These feelings were so intense that you felt the purpose of existence was for everyone to experience this. It is a feeling that gave me the insight that the universe is eternally expanding and contracting to make itself more beautiful and wonderful for us to experience.

HEAVEN'S PLACE

Heaven is where…..
   Velvet raptures touch the heart
   Like soft music through the air,
   To free our spirits to depart
   From remembrances of worldly care…..

Heaven is where…..
   The golden softness of morning dew
   Wraps the escaping twilight,
   Which changes into a hall of crimson hue
   To lead away the darkness of earthly night…..

Heaven is where…..
   Our spirits are free to depart
   Into vistas of hidden seeing,
   To explore the soul's eternal heart
   For beautiful states of re-being…..

                                         R.V.

Author's Post Reflections

What have I learned from these visions? Foremost I discovered that the belief systems we have been raised with or followed in our Earth-plane existence are irrelevant if they do not encourage us to love ourselves, each other, and the God-Source of all life. In these visions, love appeared to be the force underlying everything I saw. The best analogy, and probably the simplest one, is that love there, like the sun here, shines warmth and light on everyone without regard to one's position in life. However, in Heaven the warmth and light of love is felt not only on the outer surface of our being, but all through it, all the time.

I also learned through these visions that Heaven is multi-dimensional, and that our soul's consciousness can be transported to these other dimensions. Transportation to higher dimensions does require us to develop or "fine-tune" our spiritual bodies to the right harmonic key to emerge into that dimension. The greater the refinement of our ability to love in all its aspects, the easier it is for us to attune ourselves to enter these other exciting realms of existence. Our search for advanced spirituality and personal soul development is furthered by a desire to release the emotional states of fear, anger, hostility, and unforgivingness that we may have collected in our Earth-plane existence.

We need instead to honor the Holy Presence of God in us and others on a continual moment-to-moment basis. This will bring us immediate joy and great satisfaction, here and there. With the recognition of this honor, everyone can go "questing" for views of Heaven.

What is needed is a meditating system comfortable to the seeker. There are scores of writers focusing on this, whose publications can be found in the self-help, new age, and traditional religion sections of bookstores. Visions awaken when one has a very strong desire to experience them, and where concentration is focused on a singular trigger. This could be a special piece of music, a certain tone, a painting, or a candle against a neutral background in your home or in a religious establishment. A great deal of practice is usually involved.

The Sufi Muslim mystics, as well as the Christian mystics, have described various levels of "mystical ecstasy." This is summarized several places in Sophy Burnham's wonderful book, *The Ecstatic Journey.* These levels are called the "Orison Succession." The Orison Succession to spiritual union is an exploration of our inner consciousness to fully commit our thought patterns to visualize in steps the God Force, and the glorious beauty within every living thing.[3]

By attuning our thought patterns to focus on light changing from colors to whiteness, we create a "field energy break" similar to what a generator does in our three-dimensional world. We are now ready to go "questing" to explore the Shores of Heaven.

I believe that questing for our place in Heaven begins when we make a conscious choice to let the

---

[3] Sophie Burnham, *T.H.E. Ecstatic Journey: The Transforming Power of Mystical Experience* (New York: Ballentine Books, 1997), 180–181.

loving presence of the God Light surround us. This begins by wishing that the loving presence of this great "Force" will also occur in the lives of everyone we meet and have in our own lives. Courtesy and kindness in every behavioral action becomes much more likely when we all wish this "Loving Presence" to be near us and others.

When we wish this phenomenon to occur, we send out a "Signal Field" of projected thought from the frontal forehead area of our brain. This is much like radio waves emanating from a central broadcast tower. When our well-wishing is extended outward toward others, we greatly enhance the possibility that they will climb a step farther into higher consciousness, to begin exploring the Shores of Heaven.

Differences in age, race, religion, sex, and ethnic background become irrelevant in this beautiful exchange of sending love to others. All forms of prejudice that we hold must melt away before we can take these first steps.

In closing, I would like to share one simple "questing" activity. Picture yourself walking inside a rainbow, becoming a walking, living, breathing rainbow of light ascending upward and beyond to a whiter, brighter light. Then look beyond; concentrate on that one bright light completely surrounding you— stay in it for a while. This "White Field" may lead you to see what is beyond, and then you will be walking on the Shores of Heaven.

Cancer Survivor Park Information

This photograph depicts one of the 24 beautiful cancer survivor parks developed and financed by the R. H. Bloch Cancer Foundation. These parks are located throughout the United States and Canada; they are places that provide solace, reflection, and hope for those battling and surviving cancer. All of these parks feature inspirational plaques with messages for reflection and hope to guide visiting patients and families.

A beautiful video can be accessed on the R. H. Bloch Cancer Foundation website (http://blochcancer.org/2010/08/a-video-portrait-of-cancer-survivors-park/).

There are several unique elements in the parks that make them a great place to visit, both for cancer patients being treated and for those recovering and surviving after treatment. The parks were all well designed by talented architects, and they contain beautiful sculptures, many fashioned by a renowned sculptor, for example Victor Salmones from Mexico.

All of the Bloch parks memorialize the hope for a healthy and positive life. For everyone who goes through or passes by the parks, their beauty and significance help foster the attitude that a real possibility always exists for survival, and for those fighting cancer the parks provide encouragement to fight and win rather than surrender to cancer.

For information about cancer treatments, please visit the R. H. Bloch Foundation hotline: 1-800-433-0464.

Commentary:
Impressions Surrounding the Visions

Each image of the twelve places described in this book has a specific purpose, designed for soul elevation and growth. Each place radiates its own special level of peace, joy, and bliss. Each transmits vibrations for one's soul-self to go a step further toward greater wholeness and perfection.

These twelve heavenly places were definitively designed for raising our "consciousness of being" to a host of unrecognized potentials, the highest, no doubt, centered on finding the ways and means to uplift others toward greater soul excellence.

From the process of experiencing these twelve visions, I received the distinct impression that there are countless others, many of which you the reader may discover and experience through mystical transcendental meditation. This quest for "mind-soul-walking" into other dimensions that lie beyond carries the possibility for endless exploration, and can be the highest of spiritual endeavors for personal refinement and enlightenment.

Making the decision to grow and become better than we have been leads us into "Angelhood." As we redefine ourselves in Heaven's Light, we can move into higher zones of being. When traveling in my mind's eye to these twelve visionary places, I have occasionally observed from a distance stormy gray-dark areas of oscillating energy. These regions had a misty vibrating shield around them. I sensed that they might be zones for dwelling where vibrations were lower in frequency. These zones had places where soul-travelers perhaps of lower vibrations appeared to be entangled for a time, until they would make a sincere decision to seek greater soul perfection and excellence.

The seeking of greater soul perfection is highly dependent upon the goal of wanting to give love outwardly, and finding ways to transmit attitudes and behaviors that can awaken greater love and positive attitudes in the souls of others. This desire can immediately bring a light-stream of higher vibration for any soul to move out of a lower zone and onward to a higher zone or dimension.

Wherever we are, when we choose to focus love toward the Source that created us, and to honor that Source in everyone as being a part of that Prime Creative Source here and beyond, then no moment in our lives has a critical finality. Instead, each moment brings the potential for a new and greater perceptual awareness for us to redefine our lives for a more abundant and complete life.

More specifically, the seeking of higher perfection resides in the frequency of the decision to project love. Love in this sense is the will to transmit great affection toward the Prime Creative Source and all other living beings, to appreciate the beauty of their creation and the creative processes of all life. Having this goal opens a direct "life-line" for moving out of any dark zone here in our three-dimensional world, as well as beyond.

I found Deepak Chopra's book *How to Know God*[4] to be an outstanding guide that can help anyone who is seeking to gain a better understanding of how to enhance their potentials for spiritual excellence. A study of his brilliantly described concepts can raise our souls' vibrational levels, together, helping us to walk into a more perfect light. It's a spiritual challenge that I continually look forward to, and I hope you, dear reader, will feel the same.

---

[4] Deepak Chopra, *How To Know God, The Soul's Journey into the Mystery of Mysteries*, Harmony Books, New York, 2000.

www.ingramcontent.com/pod-product-compliance
Lightning Source LLC
Chambersburg PA
CBHW041358090426
42741CB00001B/8